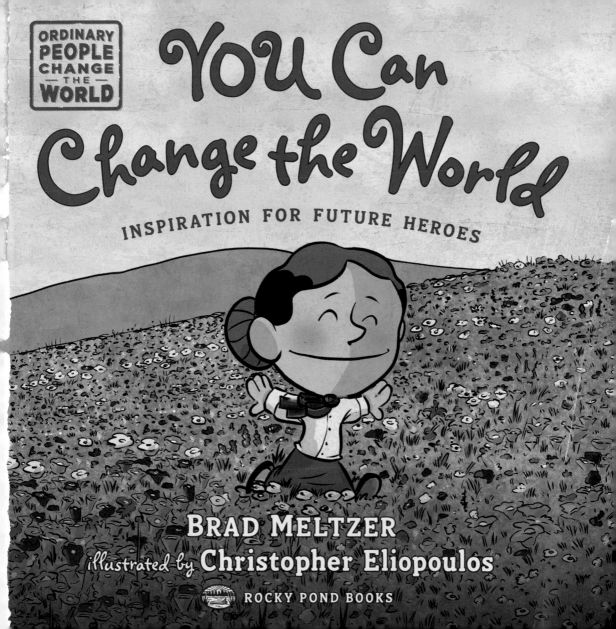

ORDINARY
PEOPLE
CHANGE
— THE —
WORLD

YOU Can
Change the World

INSPIRATION FOR FUTURE HEROES

BRAD MELTZER

illustrated by Christopher Eliopoulos

ROCKY POND BOOKS

ROCKY POND BOOKS
An imprint of Penguin Random House LLC, New York

First published in the United States of America by Rocky Pond Books,
an imprint of Penguin Random House LLC, 2024

Visit us online at PenguinRandomHouse.com.

Library of Congress Cataloging-in-Publication Data is available.

ISBN 9780593700464 • 10 9 8 7 6 5 4 3 2 1

Manufactured in China

TOPL

Design by Jason Henry • Text set in Triplex • The artwork for this book was created digitally.

Want to know the greatest secret of history?

It's that history isn't just something that goes backward.
History goes forward too.
All those great things that haven't happened yet...that's not just the future.
That's history that's *waiting* to be written.
So as your new chapter begins, here's some advice
from a few ordinary people, who, like you,
are proof that there's *no such thing* as an ordinary person.
Every life makes history. And every life is a story.
It's your turn now.

You can change the world.

In my life, I took many flights.

Every single time, there was someone who said that I wouldn't be able to do it.

Never let anyone stop you.

Whatever your dream is, chase it.

Work hard for it.

You will find it.

And I hope you'll remember that the greatest flight you'll ever take is the one no one has tried before.

Know no bounds.

I am
Albert Einstein.

Never stop asking "Why?"

Never stop trying to figure out how the world works.

And never lose that feeling of excitement as you try to find the answer.

Curiosity is one of the most powerful forces of nature.

The more questions you ask, the more answers you'll find.

And the more beauty you'll uncover in the universe.

Never stop being curious.

I am
Marie Curie.

I didn't let anyone limit what I could achieve.
It's easy to follow the crowd and do what's been done before.
But to forge your own path, you have to be daring.
Science taught me to ask questions,
    experiment,
        fail,
          try again,
            and then try some more.
You won't always find the answers you expect, and that's okay.
You will find new information, new questions, new possibilities.

Know the power
of discovery.

I am
Frida Kahlo.

My face, my clothes, the colors on my canvas—
they don't look like anyone else's,
and they shouldn't.
Art is like life.
It's messy and bold and scary and fun,
and it's all part of your picture—
a magnificent self-portrait that's uniquely yours.

The most beautiful thing is you—just as you are.

In my life, people tried to knock me down.
They tried to count me out.
But my biggest fights weren't in a ring.
They were for principles—for things I believed in.
Was I scared?
I was plenty scared.
I just didn't let it stop me.

Always fight
for what you believe.

Wherever you go in life—
whatever mountains you climb and challenges you face—
find your own way.
Make your own path.
Shatter expectations.

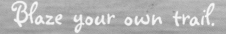

Blaze your own trail.

I am
Jane Goodall.

In your life, it will be easy to see how others
are "different" from you.
But there's so much more to gain if you instead see
how alike we all are.
All of us—all living things—share so much.
We have so many things in common.
We don't own this Earth. We share it.
When one of us is in trouble—be it human, creature,
or nature itself—we must reach out and help.
When we do, we build a bridge . . .
a bridge that will carry all of us.

We have so much in common.

Sometimes life will be hard.
When it is, look up.
See the beauty of the world and the beauty in people.
You can always find light in the darkest places.
That's what hope is.
It's a fire within you.
And when it burns bright, nothing can put it out.

Keep believing that people are truly good at heart.

I am
Neil Armstrong.

To reach the stars,
I needed to solve problems
by testing and failing, and testing and failing.
It is the key to science, and also the key to life.
It was never just one small step that got me to the moon.
It was the thousands that came before it.
Every mistake teaches you a better way forward.

Every journey begins with a first step.

I am
George Washington.

There are many ways to lead.

You can be a quiet leader, a tough leader, a bold leader.
But leadership doesn't come from charisma.
It comes from courage:
The courage to do what's right.
The courage to serve others.
The courage to go first.
Leadership isn't about being in charge.
It's about taking care of those in your charge.

Find the courage to do what no one's done before.

Think of your life as a hill that must be climbed.
There's no correct path to get to the top.
We all zigzag in our own ways.
At some point, you'll slip,
    you'll fall,
            you'll tumble back down again.
But if you get back up and keep climbing, I promise you...
You will reach the top.
There will always be obstacles.
But there will always be ways around them.

Don't let anything
stop you.

I am
Harriet Tubman.

I fought for my independence.

And once I had breathed the air of freedom,
I knew I needed to help others breathe it too.
The measure of success isn't what you achieve for yourself,
it's what you do for others.
You can make the safe choice...or the right choice.
Would you put yourself at risk to help someone else?
Would you stand up to someone mighty in order to help someone who is weak?
To answer those questions, you must follow your heart—your own north star.
It will always point you in the right direction.

Follow your north star.

I am
Abraham
Lincoln.

Strength can take many forms.
But there's nothing quite as strong as standing up
for someone who needs it.
No matter where you're from, or how little you have,
one thing that can never be taken away from you is your voice.
When you find something you believe in, use your voice.
And when you see injustice, speak louder than you've ever
spoken before.
It's the most powerful way to be heard.

Always speak your mind and speak for others.

I am
Malala Yousafzai.

I may be small, but I am mighty.
You are mighty too.
Do not be quiet!
Reading. Learning. Thinking. Speaking up.
These are gifts that are yours to use.
That's how we move the world forward.
Pick up your books and pens.
They are your most powerful weapons.

E LOVE
MALALA

RIGHT TO
EDUCATION

Education helps us all soar.

Be different!

We need people who are different.

The world doesn't get better by doing things the same way.

It gets better by creative and unconventional thinking.

We all have gifts to give.

Share what you have with the world. Share the things you love.

There's not just one right way.

The world is more beautiful for it.

Be proud to be different.

I am Jim Henson.

Goodness lives in each of us.

That's an idea that should never get old.
It starts when we're kids—when we learn some of the best things in life.
Laughing. Sharing. Imagining. Dreaming. Creating.
Never stop doing them.
And never stop being kind.
There's nothing wrong with being a do-gooder.

Keep believing and
keep pretending.

In my life, I was told to stay out of trouble,
to stay quiet,
to stay out of the way.
That's definitely the easier path.
But when you or someone else is being treated unfairly,
it's not the *right* path.
If something isn't right, or just, or fair,
you need to say something,
do something,
help those who need it.
Make some noise and move your feet.
Freedom only comes when people take action.

Go make some good trouble.

All of us are powerful in our own ways.

So how do you get to be your best self?

By practicing, sweating, and giving everything you've got.

And when you have nothing left, give more.

Most of all, in both sports and life, play fair.

Real victory doesn't come from points scored.

It comes from how you treat others in the game.

Champion equality.

People tried to knock me down.
Tried to make me feel less than I was.
Let me be clear: No one should be able to do that.
But if they try, you must stand strong.
Stand up for yourself (even if it means sitting down).

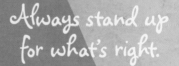

Always stand up
for what's right.

Life is not a straight path.

It curves and zigzags,
filled with surprises that are meant to be explored and discovered.
Wherever you go, go with all your heart.
Your future is yours to construct, brick by brick.
You can design it, shape it, and . . .
Build something beautiful.
Build something meaningful.
Build something that
expresses who you are.

You are the architect of your own life.

When someone hurts you,

it can be tempting to hurt them back.
You must refuse.
When someone shows you hate, show them love.
When someone shows you violence, show them kindness.
To reach our goals, we must walk the path of peace.
Whatever struggle you face, no matter how hard it gets,
you must always move forward.
I am proof of this.

Don't let anything stop your dream.

There's only one thing you gotta be in life: Yourself.
Whatever you are, be authentically that.
And the people who look, sound, or think different from you?
Love them for who they are too.
Your dreams are worth dreaming.
Your songs are worth singing.
Your story is worth telling.
Just as it is.
I see the light that shines within you.

Be proud of who you are, and don't ever limit yourself.

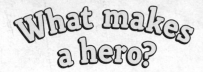

What makes a hero?

Collect them all!